THE MYSTERIOUS CAVE

MISSIONS STORIES BOOK 1

FINAL FRONTIERS FOUNDATION

© 2022 Final Frontiers Foundation, Inc. All rights reserved.

In the deep forest of India, there lives a man named Battina Babu Rao.

Since birth, he had been part of the Hindu religion. The people of this religion do not know Jesus Christ. Instead, they worship sticks, stones, snakes, and small gods and goddesses.

Battina lives in a small village in a valley, surrounded by forests and high mountains. His house is a tiny mud house with a dirt floor, and a roof made with palm branches. He does not have a lot of money, and just like other people in his small village, Battina used to go out into the forest to hunt animals.

He did not have a gun, so he would use a bow and an arrow to hunt and kill birds and small mammals. Battina would then walk a long distance to other villages to sell the birds and meat for money. That was how he survived.

One perfect day, Battina left his mud house with his bow and arrow, ready to hunt more birds and animals. It was in the middle of the day, so the sun was still up.

As he tried to hunt, he did not find any mammals or birds. And while Battina did wonder why this was happening, he did not give up. In fact, he continued to search for animals deeper and deeper into the forest. Soon, the sun started to set, and it was getting dark, so Battina decided to return home.

In the forest, there are tigers and snakes that come out in the evening to kill small animals and people too, so Battina rushed back home. As he rushed, he missed his way, and he became lost!

Battina took the wrong path, but he did not know that until he had walked a very long way and the sun was no longer in the sky. Battina found a cave, and even though it was scary, he said to himself, *'this is better than walking in the deep and dark forest.'*

Battina gathered some wood and made a fire to keep himself warm, but he stayed awake all night so that nothing would harm him. Battina remained safe, and soon, it was morning again.

As Battina was about to leave, he decided to explore the cave because it was very big and it looked ancient. In the cave, there were bones scattered around and writing with pictures on the wall.

Battina walked even deeper into the cave, and soon, he saw three skeletons that were locked up in chains. Besides the skeletons, he saw guns and bullets and then a small bag.

Battina opened the bag and brought out some papers. He sat down to read the papers, and that was when Battina learned about the miracles and teachings of Jesus Christ.

These teachings were great, and Battina took the papers home with him. His life changed greatly after that day. Battina found the address on the paper and visited it. It was a church, and the pastor led Battina to Christ.

Battina could not contain his joy, so he shared the news with all the people in his village. He taught them about Jesus and started converting them and baptizing them with water.

Battina has not stopped ever since that day. To this day in India, all Battina does is convert the people who worship animals and offer sacrifices, and he is making them see the light in the Gospel of Jesus Christ.

To the Reader:

In 1986 when I began to travel the world, seeking experienced church planters to support, I began by asking them to tell me their stories. Sometimes it was in a sticky, humid hotel room without fans. Sometimes it was on a train car so filled with people that I could not sit to write. Sometimes it was while seated on a bamboo floor in Southeast Asia, inside a mud hut on an African plain, or even while seated up against a wall on a cobblestone street in Central or South America. On several occasions, it was inside a dilapidated and freezing house in Soviet-occupied regions or a three-thousand-year-old Middle Eastern ruin. Their stories intrigued me and not only opened my eyes to see their courage but also the value of what we call national preachers.

For nearly four decades, I have longed to share these stories with children in America, hoping the desire to support national church planters through our Great Commission Fund will be planted in their hearts and grow as they mature.

The staff of Final Frontiers, led by my son Daniel and my son-in-law Michael took it upon themselves to take my dream and turn it into a reality. They picked one of my favorite stories about a preacher I met in the early 1990s in east India. A man whose story I have written and shared in scores of churches, not only in the United States but also worldwide. Now, they are sharing his story with you and your children. We want to make missions come alive in their young hearts and influence the rest of their lives, and their children, and theirs. And while our staff shares with you these amazing stories, I'll be back in other steamy hotel rooms, dugout canoes, and bombed houses and passing through three-thousand-year-old doors to sit, sip a cup of tea or coffee, and learn more stories of the most courageous preachers of our day.

These are not made-up tales. They are factual accounts about mostly still living preachers, of whom the world is not worthy. And as such, you, your children, and your grandchildren need to know about them. Be looking for upcoming issues of more preachers and stories of children blessed through our Touch a Life Child Rescue Centers. To be alerted as each is available, register at www.FinalFrontiers.world.

Be blessed.

Jon Nelms, Founder -- Final Frontiers Foundation

www.ingramcontent.com/pod-product-compliance
Lightning Source LLC
Chambersburg PA
CBHW051323110526
44590CB00031B/4450